Debbie Bonesteel Goux

EVERLASTING

WestBow
PRESS®
A DIVISION OF THOMAS NELSON
& ZONDERVAN

Bible scriptures: Scriptures taken from the Holy Bible, New International Version®, NIV®. Copyright © 1973, 1978, 1984, 2011 by Biblica, Inc.™ Used by permission of Zondervan. All rights reserved worldwide. www.zondervan. com The "NIV" and "New International Version" are trademarks registered in the United States Patent and Trademark Office by Biblica, Inc.™

WestBow Press books may be ordered through booksellers or by contacting:

WestBow Press
A Division of Thomas Nelson & Zondervan
1663 Liberty Drive
Bloomington, IN 47403
www.westbowpress.com
1 (866) 928-1240

ISBN: 978-1-9736-0464-8 (sc)
ISBN: 978-1-9736-0465-5 (e)

Library of Congress Control Number: 2017915825

Print information available on the last page.

WestBow Press rev. date: 10/25/2017

This book is dedicated with love everlasting to
my husband, my daughters, and grandchildren
who have walked this journey with me.

Our lives have encountered turbulence along the way. But I am
so thankful to God that He never gave up on us. His compass led
us to Him. I am thankful for the gifts that He has given me.

In addition, this book is written in loving memory of my
mother and father who were devout in their love for the Lord.

*But from everlasting to everlasting the LORD's love is with those
who fear him and his righteousness with their children's children.*
(Psalm 103:17, NIV Study Bible, Zondervan)

Contents

A New Walk in Faith

I am Alive in My Walk

I am alive in my walk with You.
My life is full and so brand new.
Lord I raise my voice in song.
Now I know where I belong.

I am alive in my walk with You.
Your love with me in all I do.
My joy is radiant in Your light.
There is nothing more to fight.

I am alive in my walk with You.
Your promises are so very true.
I have no more fear inside.
With You, I can always confide.

I am alive in my walk with You.
I am blessed with a different view,
That Your grace is enough for me.
My faith now shows for all to see.

Lift my Soul

Lord, lift my soul.
Yes, lift my soul.
So I can surely see
How wondrous life can be.

Lord, hear my cry.
Yes, hear my cry.
Please show me how
To change my life and now.

Lord, I am free.
Yes, I am free.
I have strength to cope.
You have brought me hope.

Lord, I have joy.
Yes, I have joy.
My life is new these days.
I forever give you praise!

A New Dance

My life seems to be on hold.
I am waiting, waiting to be told.
God, am I doing something wrong?
I struggle so, wanting to belong.

My life must mean more than this.
My negative mind I must dismiss
Speak to me, Lord, so I can hear
Your love and direction loud and clear.

I remember the refrain from long ago.
Is that all there is? It isn't, I know.
Yet I am so often plagued with doubt.
Satan takes over; God, cast him out.

I am opening my heart so very wide
So there is room for only You to abide.
Today, not tomorrow, is my chance
To start a new life; with You, a new dance.

Blessings

You enrich my life beyond compare.
If I listen, You are always there.
Your love surrounds me like a shield.
My faith unleashed; no more concealed.
Your love is the first and very last word,
Making everything clear, nothing blurred.
Your radiant presence envelopes me,
A feeling so wondrous; how can it be?
You died on the cross to save my soul,
What suffering you bore to make me whole.
I'm counting my blessings, naming each one
Thinking back to a day when there were none.
Now with your grace, my blessings abound.
My heart has been healed; a new life found.
God, thank you for this glorious new day.
Thank you for hearing me when I pray.
I am counting my blessings, yes, one by one
Counting them to remind me of all You've done.
I am blessed with assurance that You are mine
You brought me a miracle – Your love so divine.

Family

My Dad

My dad was a preacher, known at the time as a supply pastor to small churches in the surrounding area. He had an 8th grade education, which was not that unusual for many in his generation – especially those who grew up in a farming community.

Because the churches were small, Dad also had to work a full time job at the refinery to support his family of five children. In addition, he prepared for three services each week – Sunday morning, Sunday night, and Wednesday night prayer meeting.

I smile when I think of Dad's sermons. When the Holy Spirit was upon my Dad, he shouted from the pulpit, stretching out the words "Welllllll, glory!" He also sometimes stomped his feet for emphasis! He loved the Lord so.

This poem is a letter of love to my Dad. I am so proud of who he was. I love and miss him greatly.

My Dad

My dad was a preacher man and a hard worker too.
He stood in the pulpit praising and shouting words so true.
When God touched his heart, he roared like thunder.
As I think back on those days, I am amazed with wonder.
He was called to preach - he only had an 8th grade education.
He worked diligently on his sermons, with much dedication.
Dad had a second full-time job; a large family to support.
It seemed our family time with him was brief, always too short.
But I know in my heart that Dad did the best he could do.
He loved us fiercely though these words were too few.
I so wish that Dad was here with me on this very day.
I would tell him I love him - more than words can say.

Behind A Moment of Grace

A few years ago, I stayed with my granddaughter for a few days while her parents were on a business trip. My granddaughter has always been very entertaining. So I had a wonderful time with this young lady whom I love very much.

As we got ready for bed – after a discussion about my snoring - I asked her if she would like to pray. Now I was still a little uncomfortable with praying out loud. But my granddaughter began without me. I will never forget this gift of God's love – praying with my granddaughter for the first time.

A Moment of Grace

"Grandma," she said, "let's pray tonight,"
Her small face smiling in the bedroom light.
I hesitated, thinking of what I would say.
God had his plan to show me the way.

Then slowly she bowed her head to pray,
Her words of grace ending our lovely day.
She clasped her hands and closed her eyes.
She thanked God for watching over our lives.

I smiled listening to her sweet, sweet voice.
But I felt pangs of regret for my early choice.
I raised my daughters without God in mind.
I missed this precious time; I was so blind.

A Moment of Grace

The words came to me as she ended with amen.
I thanked God for the glorious day it had been.
I thanked God for the second chance he gave me.
I thanked God for his timing, his love, and mercy.

I thanked God for this sacred moment of grace.
I thanked God for this child with her innocent face.
She turned to me and said, Grandma, I love you.
God answered my prayer with these words so few.

A Family Memory

Many many years ago when I was a child, my dad sang a song in church entitled "I've Gone Too Far Upon My Journey." Folklore in the family was that a cousin had written the song. The lyrics were written in pencil on a piece of paper and my dad transcribed them to his 3X5 sermon notebook.

I found that sheet of typewritten lyrics – mistakes and all – while going through some of the papers that Dad left behind. I could immediately see and hear him singing this song in the pulpit. Dad had a deep voice. If he couldn't hit the high notes, he just sang louder!

I recently found out that this song was not written by my cousin. The original title of the song was "I'm Too Far on My Journey." But most of the lyrics were the same as those in the song we knew as "I've Gone Too Far Upon My Journey."

When I first wrote this poem a few years, I was on a different journey. But God kept pursuing me and I am so happy that I was able to write a different ending to the poem.

I've Gone too Far

Looking at old photos the other day,
This faded, yellowed page came my way.
Reading the verse, I was taken by surprise.
The longing and loss brought tears to my eyes.

Immediately I saw Dad, singing this from his heart.
An image I had forgotten, a life worlds apart.
So many of those memories have been tucked away
With the ticking of time passing day after day.

I remember times when my Mom knelt to pray,
In her bedroom as I listened from the doorway.
My parents were faithful, living in God's word.
"The Lord willing" was the message I always heard.

I've Gone too Far

My life as an adult had taken a different journey.
But the past still remained; those roots still in me.
Nostalgia came in waves, thinking of those days.
Watching my Dad serve the Lord in so many ways.

For many reasons that are too difficult to say,
I wasted so many years drifting further away,
I had gone too far, away from my Lord and Savior.
I indulged in selfishness and ungodly behavior.

But I had a strong foundation that still remained.
I turned to God to hear how much could be gained.
God's love was pouring out; He was waiting for me
To become His daughter as I was meant to be.

My Grandson

My grandson, who is almost seventeen, is unique. I know that many proud grandparents will say the same. He has great respect for men of a much older generation. During the summer, my grandson helps one of his older pals on his farm. He calls this man "Pa." One of my grandson's favorite things to do is to hang out with Pa and his friends at breakfast.

I love this about him. He is such an old soul and I am so proud of him.

My Grandson

My grandson, simply put, is like no other.
He was raised and protected by a loving mother.
He is a young man with a wonderful old soul.
He knows what he wants, seeks his own goal.

He is wise beyond his years, from a time long ago.
His maturity continues to emerge and grow.
He respects the elderly, so unusual these days.
He looks up to these men, learning their ways.

He can spin stories, telling them in great detail.
Some of them can sound like quite the fish tale!
Yet he has morals often missing in today's youth.
He lives by strong standards; he lives by truth.

He loves tradition, keeping to it in so many ways.
There's so much about him to love and praise.
God bestowed a gift on us with this young one.
I thank God for watching over my grandson.

Moments with God

A Memorial in the Road

I was sitting at a stoplight, on my way to a Bible study at church. I noticed a simple wooden cross in the median. Roadside memorials have sadly become commonplace. The simplicity of this memorial touched me. I began to think of the individual who tragically lost his or her life in that very spot. I knew I had to write about the wooden cross.

The Wooden Cross

I was at a stoplight, waiting for the light to turn green.
I looked to my left, my heart saddened by what I had seen.
A simple wooden cross was standing in the median of the road.
This cross was in memory of a life taken quickly; a story untold.
The cross stood as a tribute of love, remembrance, and pain.
I wondered if the person knew God or did she die in vain?
Was her family comforted through God's loving embrace?
Did they know if their loved one had gone to a better place?
Then I thought of another wooden cross from centuries ago.
The cross that our Savior died upon, where He suffered so.
The image of Jesus dying flashed quickly before my eyes.
He gave it all for our redemption; He died to save our lives.

The Wooden Cross

Though I have seen countless memorials on the roadside before,
Something about the one I saw today shook me to my core.
Am I living my life, using God's gifts as he meant me to do?
The cross was a sobering reminder of what I already knew.
I might have missed this moment without God's gentle voice
He was talking to me, telling me it's time to make a choice.
It is time to be different, taking steps out of my comfort zone.
My relationship with my Father will bring rewards never known.

The Country Church

The country church stood at the end of the road.
Its crumbling foundation shifted with its load.
The weathered walls were peeling and dull gray.
Seemingly the life in this church had gone away.

All the pews were now dusty; some broken apart.
Yet the altar remained - a beautiful work of art.
Imagine the souls of those who knelt there to pray,
When tears and joy flowed freely every Sunday.

A hymnal of beloved old songs lay in a pew.
Listen to hear the voices, still ringing through
The walls of the church to our heaven on high.
Hymns were raised to God in the sweet by and by.

The church appears empty but God is still there
Watching over His House with much love and care.
The steeple beckons, seen from fields all around.
In this worn holy place, peace can still be found.

Women of God

I have been blessed beyond measure to meet some wonderful women of God in my journey. This poem is an amalgamation of those women who have walked with me. Their love of God is amazing and they have been wonderful mentors to me.

A Woman of God

She exudes a wonderful aura of light.
She beams with joy in Him – eternally bright.
She lives in God's word; her Bible is frayed.
She stands on the promises that God has made.

She is a woman of wisdom, so willing to share.
She talks of the power of his grace and his care.
She quietly listens to tales of problems and woe.
She gently reminds all to give it to God and let go.

Her love for God is boundless and contagious.
She belongs to Him so she is strong and courageous.
She is a sister, a mentor, a leader, a very dear friend.
She is a woman of God, a servant without end.

God's Handiwork

God uniquely created me. He uniquely created you. God has a purpose for me and He has a purpose for you.

At times, I foolishly think I am in control. But God can truly only provide for me and give me power in His love when I surrender my will to Him.

These poems reflect a bit of my battle and what I know to be the ultimate truth. God has a plan for me. He and only He has the power to help me find my purpose. God loves me more than I could ever imagine.

My Purpose

Strength and dignity
Clothes God made for me
He whispers in my ear
Words so soft but clear.
I have a purpose for you.
Listen to Me in all you do.
I designed you so uniquely
To live for Me completely.
Your gifts are your very own.
With prayer they'll be shown.
Walk in faith daily with Me.
Your purpose will come to be.
Laugh in the face of fear.
Rest in knowing I am here.
You are wonderfully made.
Your foundation is already laid.
Live intently, starting this day.
I will guide you along the way
To discovering My plan for you.
Prepare for life that is full and new.

An Agent of Change

An agent of change is who I want to be.
So others can see Your love in me.
Living a life of joy and peace.
Trusting in You so that all worries cease.

An agent of change, how would that feel?
Making a difference; seeing Your Love heal.
My heart is brimming with desire
To walk with You and aim my life higher.

An agent of change – the thought stirs my soul.
No time to waste to achieve this goal.
I'm letting go – removing every chain,
That binds me to living with needless pain.

An agent of change – I bow my head to pray.
For Your direction to start a new day
To take those steps out of my comfort zone
To show others that with You, we are never alone.

Power in You

Fill my spirit with Your power.
Walk with me each and every hour.
Your precious love I desperately need.
God, I seek Your heavenly lead.

At times life can be so very hard.
Times I feel I must be on guard.
Fighting the worries and anxiety.
Forgetting to trust Your vision for me.

Then I hear You speak softly but clear.
Reach out to Me, child. I am here.
My burden lifts. My heart becomes light.
I can feel Your love, Your strength, Your might.

Though life's troubles will not disappear,
I know that with You, I have nothing to fear.
I will keep You first, giving You full control.
With You in charge, I am safe and whole.

What is Your Will?

God, I ask you what is Your will?
When you tell me, will I trust You?
I wonder what role I should fulfill.
When You tell me, will I trust You?

You are omniscient in all Your ways.
When You call me, will I hear You?
You have a purpose for all my days.
When You call me, will I hear You?

God, You are mighty, the King of Kings.
When You say follow Me, will I go?
Your love envelopes me, my heart sings.
When You say follow Me, yes, I will go.

My God Provides

God provides, oh yes, my God provides.
I can feel Him now, I know my God provides.
Life can bring us many trials and pain.
But there is One who can lift our soul again.
Out of the valley where sadness takes us down.
If we only believe in the King who wore the crown!
God provides, oh yes, my God provides.

I can feel Him now, I know my God provides.
He gives us courage to overcome it all.
God loves us even when we stumble and fall.
Turn your eyes toward the radiance of the Man
Who will bring you such joy; He surely can!
God provides, oh yes, my God provides.

My God Provides

I can feel Him now, I know my God provides.
Take that step to join Him for what is right.
Take that step to join Him in the light!
He will answer your call to rise above.
God will shower you with His perfect love.
God provides, oh yes my God provides.
I can feel Him now, I know my God provides.

God's Creation

Being outside in God's nature is an amazing gift. Even the most insignificant creation, such as dandelions, can be so beautiful. My words are not adequate.

For in six days the LORD made the heavens and the earth, the sea, and all that is in them, but he rested on the seventh day.
(Exodus 20:11, NIV Study Bible, Zondervan)

A Change of Seasons

The leaves are turning,
Lovely colors to see
Fall brings a yearning
For a difference in me.
Varying shades of gold
Burnt orange and red
Watching beauty unfold
Yet regrets in my head.
The fall leaves will drop,
Branches becoming bare,
God reminds me to stop
And know He is there.
New foliage will sprout,
New chances at living
God's grace is about
Freedom in forgiving.

Dandelions

Bright yellow dandelions in the grass,
Sprouting here and there, some en masse.
I pick one or two and bring them to my nose.
Memories come to me – highs and lows.

Some would argue these are just weeds.
The dandelions shed, spreading more seeds.
But as I sniff this little yellow flower,
Pictures of youth fill my mind by hour.

I think how wonderful to be carefree again,
Delighting in small pleasures with a grin.
The dandelion reminds me it can still be.
If I take time out and let my spirit be free.

A Desert View

The landscape is barren, almost nothing but sand.
Why would someone choose to live in this stretch of land?
But, as I sit here longer, my thoughts churning anew,
I see there is beauty around -this desert with a view.
A hummingbird flitters in a tree nearby.
The clear, bright shades of blue in the sky.
Even the lizard slithering along the ground.
The serenity in the desert brings a muted sound.
In the distance, the mountains stand majestic and tall.
This range, built by rocks, forms an endless wall.
I can't help but wonder what is on the other side.
But why not breathe and enjoy where I currently abide?
The chorus of birds are chirping and singing.
The chimes on the porch are gently ringing.
I'm at peace as I sit here feeling love, too.
God's presence is here in the desert with a view.

A Ball of Fire

A ball of fire blazing through the tree.
The morning light is a wonder to see.
This moment of joy starts the day ahead.
I too often take much for granted instead.

The ball of fire is a reminder to me
Just how glorious life is when I just be
In the amazing grace of Gold's holy creation.
I am thankful for this quiet celebration.

Trials and Tribulations

Loneliness

My very first venture into poetry began at a time when I was feeling lonely. Although God was waiting for me, I did not have a relationship with Him at the time. Now I look back on these words and I am thankful for God's patience. He is with me now and life is joyful.

She Didn't Cry

The years were passing her by
But she didn't cry.
She thought she had to be strong
And oh the days were long.
But she didn't cry.

She looks in the mirror
All those years but nothing clearer
Where has the time gone?
She thought of her life; so little done.
But she didn't cry.

Her time has come; her children are there
But no one else; no friends to care.
How did this happen? No love to share?
Now she cried and cried with despair.
The years had passed her by.

How Am I Worthy?

My favorite hymn shouts it in prose.
Up from the grace, Christ arose.
How am I worthy of His horrific pain?
Christ drenched in blood, covered in stain.
Christ died for me to make me whole.
He only wanted to save my soul.
How am I worthy of his sacrifice?
Christ bore my sin, an ultimate price.
I think of the tomb, only linens I see.
Christ arose, reigning with victory!
How am I worthy of His love so amazing?
I am overcome with joy and praising.
I am worthy because He forgives me.
I am worthy because of His mercy.
I am worthy because of His great grace.
With Him is my haven, my purpose, my place.

A Hit and Run Prayer

In my walk of faith, I have not always been disciplined in seeking God first. I have allowed distractions to get in the way. On busy days, I call it "A Hit and Run Prayer." I know that taking time in the morning to talk with God and read his Word makes all the difference in the world as to how my day will be.

God can't have the relationship with me that He wants to have if I only give him a couple of minutes in the morning before I rush out into the world. He gave me these words to summarize how life can be when everything else is put first above God.

A Hit and Run Prayer

Another day, another hit and run prayer.
So much to do in the big world out there.
God I need your blessing to start the day.
Please make it fast so I can be on my way.

Tomorrow will be different, really I swear.
Now what am I going to do with this hair?
God of all creation, you are the Great I am.
Gotta check my email – what is this spam?

The day has flown by; I flop on the couch.
I check the lottery – no win again – ouch!
I change TV channels so, so many times,
Nothing but violence, madness, and crimes.
I'll pray in the morning; that will be enough.

A Hit and Run Prayer

As I head to bed, I think I really should pray.
But I'm just too tired to think of what to say.
God doesn't want to hear the same old stuff.
I'll pray in the morning; that will be enough.

Morning comes. I'll be late if I don't hurry.
I am starting this day with anxiety and worry.
God can You help me? What is your will?
There is just no time to stop, pray and be still.

I will pray tonight when there is more time.
Gotta go – it's the corporate ladder I climb.
God I am sorry. I promise I will squeeze you in.
It is just so strange how empty my life has been.

That Four-Letter Word

That four-letter word fills my mind.
Why oh why can't I leave it behind?
It is harmful and sinful to say the least.
It is overwhelming - this ugly beast.

Fear strangles me, suffocating my joy.
Fear lodges in my brain, ready to deploy.
Satan laughs when he sees my anxiety.
I cry to God – please, please release me.

Fear is the absence of faith, I am told.
With faith, I'm an overcomer and bold.
Do I doubt my faith in our God above?
Do I doubt his powerful redeeming love?

He tells me He leaves his peace to me.
Why can't I embrace this gift and see
That God has a plan beyond my control?
That God wants my heart and my soul?

His words come to me- No need to be afraid!
Remove those barriers you have made.
Replace your fear with the five letter word.
With faith-not fear- My voice can be heard.

A Child's Lens

I lived a life encased in doubt and fear.
I wasn't good enough said the mirror.
I shut God out thinking He's not for me.
I thought without Him I could be free.

Through a child's lens, I had a narrow view
Of a life with God - what I thought I knew.
In my mind, I looked for something more.
I took a different path, thinking I would soar!

So I closed my heart to hearing GOD's voice.
I lived life on my own without Him as my choice.
Then trials and fear began to fold in on me.
My mind was in turmoil, days full of misery.

One snowy day, God said it is now time.
I can bring you peace, a feeling sublime.
I went to church, hungry for so much more.
I was surrounded by love just inside the door.

I now see God through a different lens.
I see love, forgiveness, and His power to cleanse
My doubts, my fears, my sadness, and my sins.
As I open my eyes to God, a beautiful life begins.

Veteran's Day

One day is not enough
To recognize your years
Of sacrifices unimaginably tough
Love of country overriding fears.

No one can ever doubt
Your fight for our freedom.
Your loyalty remains devout
Your passion glowing like a beacon.

You fiercely defend, vocal and proud,
Our country's democratic rule.
You stand upright, never bowed.
A veteran who knows the price is cruel.

How can I ever thank you
For being the man you are.
A veteran with patriotism so true.
An example without par.

You will always have my heart.
I love what is in your soul.
I am so very proud of your part
In keeping this country whole.

For my Dad and my husband, Chuck.

Decoration Day

My parents called it Decoration Day
Each year we placed flowers at the sites
Of family members who had gone away.

As I grew, I also came to understand
That this day means so much more.
We honor those who fought for our land.

Far too many have given their lives
For our country and for those abroad,
Sacrificing so our freedom survives.

Their bravery demands honor and respect.
These lives so young, gone far too soon
Their love of country we must never forget.

Bless those who hearts led them to fight.
Whether Decoration Day or Memorial Day,
May God always protect us with His Might.

God's Army

As children in Sunday School, we sang a simple song,
Shouting "I'm in the Lord's army" so loud and strong!
Those days of belting out this chorus are long gone.
Yet there are battle lines that are still being drawn.

Satan wages a ferocious war every minute of the day.
He wants us to pick his side, to follow him and his way.
He taunts us – what is really wrong with his choice?
He tries to drown out the Lord with his cunning voice.

But God overcomes Satan's sly, underhanded style.
His tactics are love, grace and mercy – no meaningless guile.
His expert strategy brings freedom from guilt and shame.
Our God is tenacious; He is not playing a shallow game.

He will never give up on us - He wants us to serve in His army.
He created us to be a soldier for Him – to be everything we can be.
God is the Great Victor who brings contentment and peace.
With God on our side, life is eternal and will never cease.

About the Author

Debbie's poetry often reflects her life's journey, battling to be in control while running away from God. Debbie grew up in a Christian family but spent much of her adult life thinking that the 'God thing' wasn't for her. Seven years ago, Debbie stopped running and became a daughter of the King, developing a relationship with God. Debbie evolved from a young mother to a corporate career in Learning and Development. However, writing has been her passion throughout her life. After many years of travel as an Air Force spouse, Debbie currently lives in Fort Smith, Arkansas. Debbie shares her home with her husband Chuck and the ruler of the household, Lily the kitty. Debbie and Chuck have a blended family of four children and 8 grandchildren.

Printed in the United States
By Bookmasters